Anchorage

Anchorage

A Downtown America Book

Joseph Oberle

Dillon Press, Inc.   Minneapolis, MN 55415

To Lora, who introduced me to Anchorage

Acknowledgments

The author would like to thank the following people for their generous help in creating this book: Richard and Joyce Dickerman, Mark Thissen, Jeff Osborn, Sherry Tollefson, Melissa Anderson, Cynthia Anderson, Diane Brenner, Jim Severson, and Lora Polack.

The photographs are reproduced through the courtesy of Melissa Anderson, Joseph Oberle, Mark Thissen, the Anchorage Convention and Visitor's Bureau, and the Anchorage Museum of History and Art.

Library of Congress Cataloging-in-Publication Data

Oberle, Joseph.
  Anchorage / Joseph Oberle.
    p. cm. — (A Downtown America book)
  Summary: Introduces Anchorage, Alaska, its history, neighborhoods, people, attractions, and festivals.
  ISBN 0-87518-420-0 : $12.95
  1. Anchorage (Alaska)—History—Juvenile literature. 2. Anchorage (Alaska)—Description—Guide-books—Juvenile literature. [1. Anchorage (Alaska)] I. Title. II. Series.
F914.A5024 1990
979.8'3—dc 20   89-26068
                                    CIP
                                      AC

Dillon Press, Inc., 242 Portland Avenue South
Minneapolis, Minnesota 55415

Printed in the United States of America
1 2 3 4 5 6 7 8 9 10 99 98 97 96 95 94 93 92 91 90

About the Author

Joseph Oberle has long been fascinated by the majestic natural beauty of Alaska and the frontier spirit of the people of Anchorage. Through trips to the city and his close ties with Anchoragites, he has watched the city grow and change in good times and bad. Oberle has worked as an editor for a number of magazines and has written articles for numerous publications. He has served as a contributing writer and editor for a recently published book.

Contents

Fast Facts about Anchorage

Anchorage: Air Crossroads of the World

Location: South-central coast of Alaska, at the tip of a large bay called Cook Inlet; the Chugach Mountains lie to the east of the city, Knik Arm to the northwest, and Turnagain Arm to the southwest

Area: The Municipality of Anchorage covers 1,955 square miles (5,063 square kilometers) and includes the nearby smaller communities of Eagle River, Chugiak, Birchwood, Peters Creek, Eklutna, and Girdwood

Population (1988 estimate*): Municipality of Anchorage, 230,000

Major Population Groups: Whites, blacks, native Alaskans, Asians, and South Pacific islanders

Altitude: *Highest*—Bashful Peak, 8,005 feet (2,442 meters); *Lowest*—sea level

Climate: Average temperature is 13°F (-11°C) in January, 58°F (14°C) in July; average annual precipitation is 15 inches (38 centimeters)

Founding Date: 1914, incorporated as a city in 1920

City Flag: City seal on a yellow-gold background

City Seal: Within a circle, the shank of a large anchor runs down through the middle of a sailing ship, with an airplane flying above the ship at the right; *Anchorage* appears at the top of the circle and *Alaska* at the bottom

Form of Government: Anchorage is a municipality governed by a mayor, an 11-member elected municipal assembly, and a city manager appointed by the mayor

Important Industries: Transportation, communication, wholesale and retail trade, tourism, and government, which includes the military and public schools and hospitals

*Official 1990 Bureau of the Census figures available in 1991-1992.

Festivals and Parades

February: Fur Rendezvous; Northern Lights Invitational; Winter Festival in Eagle River

March: Iditarod Trail Sled Dog Race; St. Patrick's Day Parade

April: Alaska Native Youth Olympics

June: Summer Solstice Festival, Mayor's Midnight Sun Marathon; Kite Day; Alaska Renaissance Festival; Alaska Women's Run; Basically Bach Festival; Midnight Sun Balloon Classic

July: Freedom Days Festival; Chugiak-Eagle River Bear Paw Festival

August: Alaska State Fair in Palmer; Scottish Highland Games

September: Oktoberfest

October: Quiana Alaska

November: Great Alaska Shootout; Symphony of Trees; Christmas Tree Lighting Ceremony

December: Seawolf Hockey Classic

For further information about festivals and parades, see agencies listed on page 57.

United States

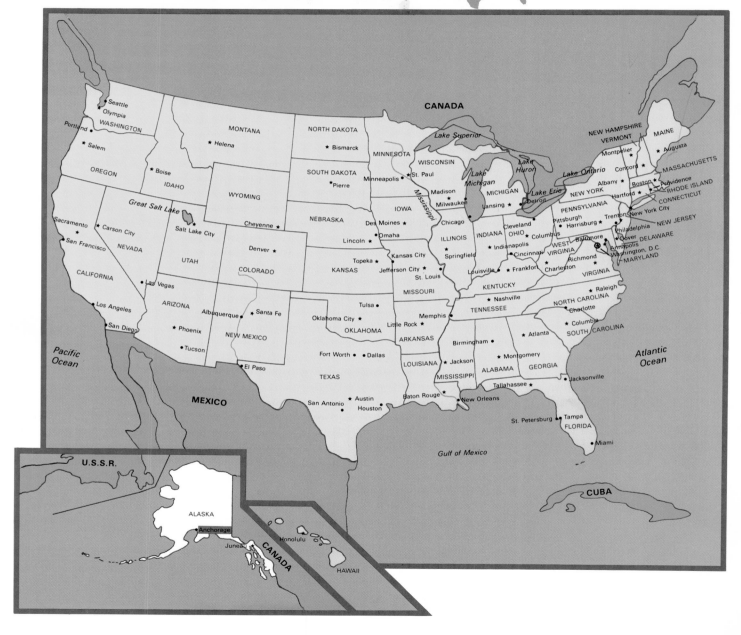

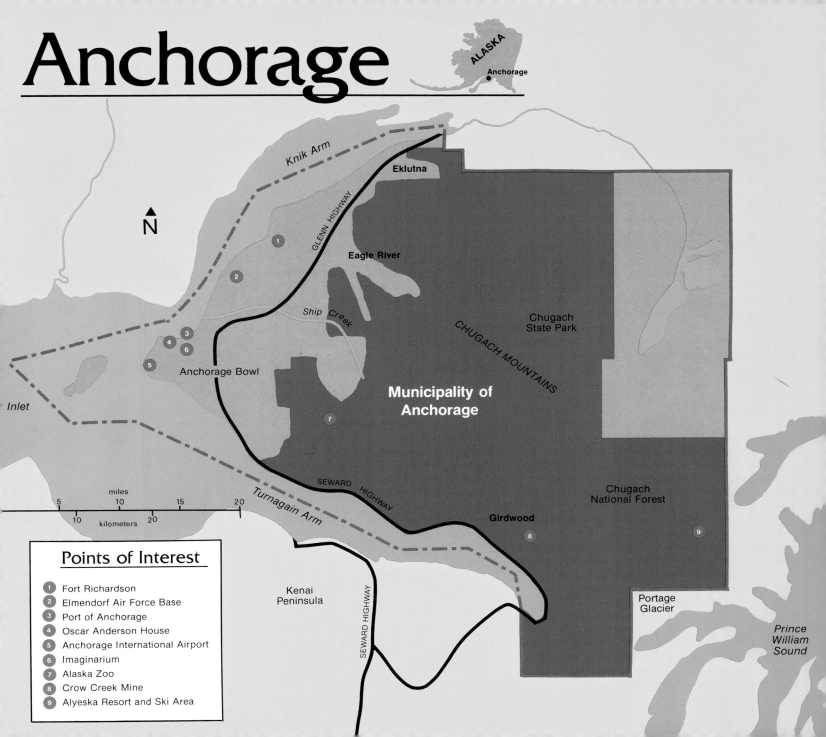

Anchorage

ALASKA
Anchorage

Knik Arm

Eklutna

GLENN HIGHWAY

Eagle River

Ship Creek

1

2

3
4   6
5

Anchorage Bowl

7

**Municipality of
Anchorage**

Chugach
State Park

CHUGACH MOUNTAINS

Chugach
National Forest

Inlet

SEWARD HIGHWAY

Turnagain Arm

Girdwood

8

9

miles
5   10
10   15
10   kilometers   20
20   15
20

Kenai
Peninsula

SEWARD HIGHWAY

Portage
Glacier

*Prince
William
Sound*

Points of Interest

1   Fort Richardson
2   Elmendorf Air Force Base
3   Port of Anchorage
4   Oscar Anderson House
5   Anchorage International Airport
6   Imaginarium
7   Alaska Zoo
8   Crow Creek Mine
9   Alyeska Resort and Ski Area

A Frontier City

Beyond the boundaries of most American cities there is room to expand. In Anchorage, Alaska, there is only room to explore. Pushed up against the two arms of Cook Inlet by the Chugach Mountains, this biggest city in the United States's largest state has the features that dreams of adventure are made of. Many of the modern pioneers who live in this frontier city came seeking an adventure they couldn't find anywhere else.

Anchorage is surrounded by natural wonders. Mountains tower over the city like black and white skyscrapers, and the weather highlights the land's beauty with each changing season. About half an hour from town lie some of Alaska's most famous glaciers. Near downtown is Earthquake Park, a reminder of the United States's worst earthquake,

Anchorage lies between the two arms of Cook Inlet.

A biker rides along a coastal path during the long daylight hours of summer in Anchorage.

which shook Anchorage in 1964. The nearby wilderness is home to moose, bears, and other wild animals.

Anchorage is a city of opposites. Winter days have, at the most, five and a half hours of sunlight, while in summer there is enough daylight to play baseball until nearly midnight. Downtown is busy and modern, full of people and traffic, yet the traffic is often muddy pickup trucks with drivers who wear flannel shirts and blue jeans. The same people who ride dogsleds during the day can go to the opera at night. And the mirrored glass buildings of the city are overshadowed by some of the highest mountains in North America.

Anchorage is located on the south-central Alaskan coast at the tip

Buildings of downtown Anchorage rise on a bluff along the shore of Knik Arm.

of a large bay called Cook Inlet. It lies in a valley sometimes called the Anchorage Bowl. Anchorage and a number of smaller communities have joined to form the Anchorage Municipality, which spreads in a V-shape up the valley. But the main part of the city stands on a triangle of land that extends into the inlet. This triangle divides the inlet: the northern arm is called Knik, and the southern arm is known as Turnagain.

Beluga whales can sometimes be spotted swimming up and down the

Knik Arm to feed. During high tide, Anchorage residents like to windsurf along Turnagain Arm. During low tide, water leaves much of Turnagain, and it becomes a sea of mud.

Anchorage sits on a geological plate—the earth's crust, or upper layer, is divided into plates—that is part of the Ring of Fire. This explosive area surrounds the Pacific Ocean and often has violent volcanoes and earthquakes. Mount Redoubt and Mount Spurr are two active volcanoes visible to Anchoragites.

Looking north across the Knik Arm, Mount McKinley, the highest peak in North America, can be seen on a clear day. Yet a hiker would have to travel more than 150 miles (241 kilometers) to reach it.

The mountains nearer to the city provide plenty of activity for the people of Anchorage. Snow caps the mountains for much of the year, making the area a frosty white paradise for visitors and local residents. In the winter, Anchoragites ski downhill in the nearby mountains, and ski cross-country on trails that run right through the city. They also ice-skate in town, and race out of the city on their snowmobiles and dogsleds.

Four mountain ranges protect Anchoragites from the harsh weather that might be expected in a city so close to the Arctic Circle. To the east and south, the Chugach and Kenai mountains shelter the city from much of the rain that comes from the Gulf of Alaska. To the north, the Talkeetna

The mountains near Anchorage provide excellent sites for downhill skiing.

Mountains and Alaska Range block blasts of arctic air. The warm waters of the North Pacific Current, which flow across the ocean near Alaska's southern coast, also help to make the winter less bitterly cold than many areas farther south.

In Alaska, winter begins in October and can last until mid-April. Anchoragites must learn to live with seemingly endless days of winter darkness. If they are not careful, they may suffer from "cabin fever," the feeling of being cut off from the rest of the world for too long. To help people keep their spirits high, residents hold festivals such as the annual Fur Rendezvous in February.

Indoors, where most of the winter is spent, some Anchoragites spend many hours watching television. Others pass the time at local bars; in fact, Anchorage has a high rate of alcoholism. People who drink too much can cause trouble for the city, especially during the winter. By April, residents wait eagerly for warm weather.

When summer finally comes, 20 hours of sunshine create different problems. In the summer, Anchoragites can have a hard time getting to bed! At its peak, the sun shines as late as midnight, and children play outside as long as the daylight lasts.

These problems are minor compared to the opportunities for fun this summer climate provides. The cool temperatures are perfect for exploring the beautiful Anchorage countryside. Anchoragites fish for pink

salmon in Ship Creek near downtown, ride bikes through Earthquake Park, or hike the foothills of the Chugach Mountains.

The good of Anchorage's climate must outweigh the bad, since more than half of the state's population lives there. Many businesses that serve Alaska have their headquarters in Anchorage, and its port is the major unloading site for supply ships that bring food and other goods to the rest of the state. Thousands of Anchoragites also work for the oil industry. Since the 1970s, the promise of jobs in oil businesses has brought many newcomers to the city from the "Lower 48" states.

Anchorage is sometimes called the Air Crossroads of the World.

Anchoragites and visitors enjoy catching fish like this huge salmon.

Planes flying the polar route between the United States and Asia and between Asia and Europe stop in the city to refuel. The city is also a starting point for flights into Alaska's "bush," the remote wilderness that can't be reached by car. Bush pilots fuel their planes for trips to isolated villages, or for flights in search of the state's wildlife.

Airplanes are a familiar sight in Anchorage, especially the fighter planes from Elmendorf Air Force Base and Fort Richardson, an army post. The city is an important U.S. defense center because it is close to the Soviet Union. Thousands of military servicemen and women call Anchorage home during their two- to four-year tour of duty.

Tourists make up another large group of visitors to the city. Hundreds of thousands come to Anchorage each year to fish, hunt, and explore the beautiful wilderness near the city. Alaskans from other parts of the state also come to Anchorage to shop and enjoy the city's nightlife, museums, festivals, and performing arts.

Anchorage's cultural heritage is as strong as it is varied. More native Alaskans live in Anchorage than in any village in the state, but blacks, Asians, and South Pacific Islanders are also active in city life. Many children in Anchorage's schools are taught in bilingual programs—classes where English and another language are used—because they speak one of

Rows of planes line part of the busy airport near downtown Anchorage.

the more than 100 different languages heard in the city.

Although it is only about 80 years old, Anchorage is every bit a hustling, bustling, modern American city. It has natural beauty for the explorer and big-city excitement for the sophisticated. It is a young city, still experiencing growing pains, yet it is strong from a pioneer spirit used to hardship. Anchorage is a city of adventure, like no other place on earth.

Seward's Folly

From the very start, Alaska has seemed to outsiders to be a difficult place to live. People saw it as cold, wild, and not very inviting. Because of this reputation, Anchorage has grown in spurts—people flock to the city when it offers jobs, and leave in more difficult times. War, earthquakes, and economic changes have all contributed to the boom-bust-boom cycle of Anchorage's history.

Yet after every setback, the determined Anchoragites have put the pieces of their city back together.

The first people to live in the area where Anchorage is today were the Athabaskan Indians. The Athabaskans were hunters who moved around with the seasons to find the caribou, moose, and rabbits they used for food, shelter, and clothing. They traded with the Aleuts from the

Colorful spirit houses were built by Athabaskan Indians in the cemetery next to Saint Nicholas Russian Orthodox church in Eklutna.

Sea otters swim in the waters of Cook Inlet.

Aleutian Islands and the Pacific Coast Eskimos. They also traded with small groups of Russian fur traders who had sailed up the inlet and set up camps along its shores. The traders came in search of the furs of sea otters and other fur-bearing animals.

In 1799, Russia established the Russian American Company in Alaska, which was then known as *Russian America*. This trading company was the only governing power in Alaska during the next 68 years. Russian traders set up a small settlement,

Eklutna, on the Knik Arm, northwest of present-day Anchorage. Although only a small number of Russians lived there, missionaries converted many of the local Indians to the Russian Orthodox religion.

In 1778, before the Russians had established settlements in Alaska, a group of English explorers had sailed into the waters near Anchorage. They had come in search of a northwest passage—a sea route between the Atlantic and Pacific oceans. The captain, James Cook, had named the bay Cook Inlet and traded supplies with the Indians. Because the inlet did not offer passage to the ocean, Cook had never returned, and Alaska remained a Russian territory.

In 1867, the United States bought

A monument to Captain Cook faces the sea in Anchorage.

Alaska from Russia. Without Congress's approval, Secretary of State William H. Seward hastily purchased the 586,400 square miles (1,518,776 square kilometers) of land for $7,200,000—less than two cents an acre. Americans who opposed buying this huge territory began to call Alaska *Seward's Folly* and *Seward's Icebox*. Yet it has gone down in history as one of the greatest land purchases ever made.

At the time, few people realized the great prize that Alaska would become. To the American people, it was a vast and frozen wilderness, all rugged country and wild animals—certainly no place to live. Nearly 50 years later, in 1912, Congress made Alaska a U.S. territory. Two years afterward, the U.S. government decided to build a railroad across the territory to open up the rugged and mineral-rich Alaskan interior.

The railroad commission needed a construction camp midway between the railroad's end points of Seward on the southeast coast and Fairbanks in inland Alaska, and they chose the site where Anchorage is now. A small settlement called Ship Creek was already located there. Before the construction crew arrived, only a small number of settlers lived in Ship Creek. But news of the Alaska Railroad spread quickly, and by April 1915, the settlement boasted a population of more than 2,000 eager job-seekers.

Although the new town was little

In the early days of Anchorage, log buildings rose next to the tents of the first settlers.

more than a group of tents, more permanent buildings were soon built. A post office was installed, and the railroad commission sold land sites to the new settlers. The tents became a town, and the townspeople chose the name *Anchorage* because of the many boats with railroad supplies that anchored in Cook Inlet.

People from all over America and Europe arrived, looking for work. The boom town grew rapidly, to a peak of 7,000 residents. By the end of the year, it had become a comfortable

Dogsleds delivered the mail to Anchoragites in the snow on December 9, 1915.

small town, complete with restaurants, stores, a theater, and an ice cream parlor. The railroad commission, which governed the town, built the first school and houses for its high-ranking employees.

Early Anchorage residents often had to be creative. Joe Spenard, who owned one of the city's only automobiles, also used it as a taxi and fire truck. Later that year, Spenard opened Anchorage's first resort along the shores of a lake that he quickly named Lake Spenard.

World War I caused hardship in Anchorage. Most of the town's residents were young men who worked on the railroad, and many of them volunteered to fight in the U.S. armed forces. By mid-1917, the population dropped to near 1,850, and it remained small for the next two decades. No other industries developed to attract new residents.

In 1920 Anchorage was still a frontier town, with unpaved roads that clogged with mud when springtime came. For eight years, the only law and order in the town was Harold Staser, a U.S. marshal. But the Alaska Railroad, which was finished in 1923, provided jobs for many residents, and the city was trying to become modern. The next year, radio station KFQD—Alaska's first radio station—began broadcasting.

Anchorage's next big spurt of growth happened during World War II, when the U.S. government built two large military bases just outside of town. Fort Richardson and Elmendorf Air Force Base brought thousands of soldiers to Anchorage. Many of them stayed on after the war to settle on homesteaded land.

The biggest change Anchorage has ever experienced began in the summer of 1957, when the Richfield Oil Company discovered oil in Cook Inlet. Oil companies began moving into the city, bringing jobs and money.

The next year was also important—Congress voted to make Alaska the 49th U.S. state on June 30, 1958. Anchoragites celebrated by taking the day off from work and building a 50-ton bonfire in Delaney Park, near downtown. On January 3, 1959, the oil-rich wilderness of Alaska became an official member of the Union, and

During the 1964 earthquake, Fourth Avenue in Anchorage dropped below street level along with cars and parts of nearby buildings.

Seward's Folly started to make more sense.

Fueled by the booming oil business, Anchorage grew rapidly. But the city's good fortune ended suddenly on March 27, 1964. On Good Friday, two days before Easter, the most pow-

erful earthquake ever recorded in North American history struck the Anchorage area. The quake lasted five minutes, and was strong enough to cause tidal waves as far away as Hawaii. Large sections of the city were destroyed—parts of downtown dropped 20 feet (6.1 meters) below street level. Houses along Cook Inlet fell into the water. In Anchorage alone, the earthquake left nine people dead and caused $300 million in damage.

The city recovered quickly and rebuilt the downtown area with bigger and more modern buildings. Seagoing traffic increased at the port, and many new businesses moved to the city. When more oil was discovered on Alaska's North Slope in 1968, people rushed to Anchorage from all over the United States. The new oil fields, and the construction of the Trans-Alaska Pipeline across the state, created many high-paying jobs. All the new workers and businesses caused the city to grow so fast that

in 1975 Anchorage and nearby smaller towns formed the Municipality of Anchorage. The municipality is run by a mayor, an 11-member municipal assembly, and an appointed city manager.

Unfortunately, as is true with any boom town, sooner or later Anchorage had to experience a bust. In the mid-1980s, when the price of oil fell sharply, the city's businesses and people suffered. Many Anchoragites lost their jobs and had to move away when they could no longer afford their house payments. Others stayed, but slowly became poorer and poorer.

To recover from this setback, the city began to look for other means to keep growing. Anchorage is now encouraging visitors from around the

world to enjoy its magnificent scenery, sports and recreation, festivals, and cultural life. In recent years, tourism has become one of the city's largest industries.

Early in 1989, an event happened that could affect both the tourism and the oil industry in Anchorage and throughout Alaska. A large oil tanker, the *Exxon Valdez*, ran aground in Prince William Sound, to the east of Anchorage. Millions of barrels of oil spilled into the sea. The oil has spread across a huge area of the Alaskan coast and killed thousands of seabirds, sea otters, and other sea creatures. Anchoragites are concerned that

tourists might stay away because of the oil spill. Some residents also fear that the opening of new oil fields in Alaska may be delayed or canceled because of concerns about damage to the environment.

In the past, the people who made the long journey to Anchorage ended up staying, and this ever-changing gateway to Alaska will attract more people once more. Perhaps those who now come to Anchorage will see what William Seward saw in Alaska many years ago. Perhaps they will see the beauty of this young and plentiful land, and will dream of the riches it has yet to offer.

Visitors from around the world take trips on cruise ships along the Alaskan coast.

3

A Pioneer Spirit

Transportation helped build Anchorage. The building of the Alaska Railroad created the city, the industry brought by ships has caused it to grow, and the planes that fill its skies have connected it to the rest of Alaska and the world. In modern Anchorage, another vehicle has become important—the automobile. Anchorage is so large and spread out that a car is necessary to travel to many parts of the city. Most families have two cars, some even three—after that, they may start thinking about a plane!

The Municipality of Anchorage covers 1,955 square miles (5,063 square kilometers), an area larger than the state of Rhode Island and four times as large as Los Angeles. Within its borders are large stretches of parkland and open areas that connect the outlying communities such

Snow-covered mountains rise behind the bright lights of Anchorage.

Tall buildings stand not far from this older house near downtown Anchorage.

as Girdwood and Eagle River to downtown and the main city.

Anchorage sprawls across so much territory because it has grown quickly at times in its history. People moving into the city could always find open spaces on which to build.

As a result, new communities have spread outward from the original settlement, rather than building upward. The original town, though, has grown into a busy downtown area where historic houses are mixed with tall, modern buildings.

Downtown Anchorage, built on a bluff along the shore, reflects its beautiful skyline in the waters of the Knik Arm. Its glass and steel skyscrapers house offices and businesses where thousands of Anchoragites make their living. Historic Fourth Avenue—which was split wide open by the earthquake of 1964—is the main street in downtown and a popular center for shopping. Many of the buildings that line this street were built when Anchoragites were recovering from the disaster, but others survived the quake.

On downtown streets, tiny, one-story frame houses built by the railroad commission stand in the shadow of skyscrapers, including the tallest building in Alaska, the 21-story ARCO Tower. Some of the houses are homes for Anchoragites, while others have been changed to be used as office space. The most important ones have been restored to their original form and now serve as historic sites or museums.

Anchoragites have recently begun serious efforts to preserve their past. The first permanent frame house was built in the city in 1915. Its owner, Oscar Anderson, lived in the house until 1974. When he died, the house was given to the city and restored as a museum. Like many other historic houses, it had to be moved from its original location to make way for new skyscrapers. Today, it stands on Cook Inlet just below downtown, at the center of a small park.

The Oscar Anderson house preserves part of Anchorage's early history.

While the historic buildings draw some people downtown, others come for the shopping. Many downtown shops feature the jade, ivory, and soapstone carvings of native Alaskans. They also display the paintings or photography of modern Alaskan artists who try to capture the natural beauty of the area.

Historic Ship Creek flows into Cook Inlet just north of downtown, and Westchester Lagoon borders the southwest corner of downtown. The lagoon is a protected area for migrating birds. In the summer, ducks and other birds nest along its shore, and in the winter, Anchoragites skate across the ice. One of Anchorage's main roads, Minnesota Drive, crosses the lagoon, connecting downtown to newer neighborhoods.

Because Anchorage has grown so rapidly, the city has developed another "downtown" called Midtown. This spread-out area of shopping malls, parking lots, office buildings, and apartments stretches south of Westchester Creek and east of Cook Inlet. Midtown attracts many of the Alaskans who come to the city from the rest of the state.

To the east of Midtown lies the neighborhood of Mountain View. Here the campuses of Alaska Pacific

A native Alaskan artist carves a finely etched design in an ivory tusk.

University (APU) and the University of Alaska, Anchorage (UAA) stand back-to-back in a peaceful wooded setting. Students from all over the world attend these two universities, which offer both graduate and undergraduate programs. While UAA is part of the statewide university system, APU is a private college.

Many students and military personnel from nearby Fort Richardson and Elmendorf Air Force Base live throughout the Mountain View and neighboring Muldoon areas. In these neighborhoods, low-cost housing units such as apartments and trailer courts are common. Most of them were built quickly to house the large numbers of job-seekers that arrived in the city during the 1970s.

Each year large numbers of Anchoragites leave to seek work elsewhere, and others move to the city to pursue their dreams. The population is young—the average age is 28, and almost three-fourths of the people are under the age of 40. As they get older, some Anchoragites leave to move to warmer climates where the winters are shorter. Many, though, are caught by the city's spell, and stay through good times and bad ones.

Well-to-do Anchoragites build their homes in the Hillside area at the southern end of the Anchorage Bowl. Residents cannot drive straight from Muldoon to Hillside. Instead, they must circle around the Campbell Creek Resource Lands, a protected area for wildlife at the foot of the

A moose and her calf enjoy a breakfast of birch branches in the yard of a home in Hillside.

Chugach Mountains. This area is the largest plot of undeveloped land within the city. Sometimes wildlife from the resource lands stray into the city—homes in Hillside have served more than one meal of birch branches to a hungry moose and her calf.

As Anchorage grows, people are building their homes on the mountainsides east of Hillside. These new homes have steep driveways and a breathtaking view of the city below.

Another popular neighborhood stretches along the shore of Turnagain

Arm. In recent years, residents there have been involved in an unusual dispute concerning land rights. The 1964 earthquake caused some houses, and the land beneath them, to be dumped into the water. After the quake, the area had a different shoreline. Some of the former homeowners would like to rebuild their houses, but those now on the shore don't want to give up their view.

Many scientists and geologists believe that another major earthquake could occur in Anchorage, and they fear it could destroy many of the buildings built on the bluffs by Cook Inlet. Others disagree. When downtown was rebuilt, they explain, the bluffs were strengthened with buttresses and are now safe.

Anchorage International Airport is also built along the shores of Cook Inlet, on the tip of the triangle that splits the inlet into Knik and Turnagain arms. There are many lakes in this part of the city. Hundreds of colorful floatplanes land on and take off from Lake Hood and Lake Spenard. The two lakes are connected by a channel and together form the largest floatplane base in the world. Jewel Lake, farther south, has a popular swimming beach.

The Municipality of Anchorage extends for miles up both arms of the inlet. Two highways lead out of the Anchorage Bowl. Seward Highway runs south, connecting the small communities of South Anchorage and Girdwood to the rest of the city.

A floatplane soars over Anchorage.

Following this highway farther south, drivers pass a ski resort, a gold mine, and several glaciers on their way down the Kenai Peninsula.

Glenn Highway runs to the north, and it is used by the commuters who work in downtown Anchorage but live in the growing community of Eagle River. Many people who work for the oil companies have flocked to the newly built homes in this area.

At the northern tip of the Municipality of Anchorage is Eklutna, a

village that still displays its Russian heritage. This small community features the oldest building in the municipality. The Saint Nicholas Russian Orthodox church was built between 1845 and 1870 by Athabaskan Indians for the Russian missionaries. In its cemetery, colorful "spirit houses" have been built over the graves as memorials. The houses are an Athabaskan Indian tradition, but they are topped with the Russian Orthodox cross.

Today, Anchorage is home to people of many different backgrounds. People have come to the city seeking their fortune, following a dream, or just looking for a beautiful spot to live. Many people have also left—some because of the cold, others because their dream died. The people who remain reflect the pioneer spirit that built the city. Anchoragites have much to be proud of, and their strong spirit will help them survive whatever changes lie ahead.

These visitors to Anchorage have stopped at historic Crow Creek Mine near Girdwood to pan for gold.

4

The Foothills of Adventure

Wherever Anchoragites wake up in their city, they are reminded of the beautiful countryside in which they live. The towering Chugach Mountains are always in sight. When the wind whispers across the snow-covered crests, they seem to beckon anyone within earshot to come and explore an Alaskan adventure.

Adventure in Alaska takes many forms, whether it's a trip to the nearby wilderness or a city-wide celebration in the streets of Anchorage. Adventure can also happen in any weather, and the city's most well known festival takes place in February.

The Fur Rendezvous, or Fur Rondy as it is fondly called, is the biggest festival in Alaska, and one of the 10 largest in the United States. Many of the festival's more than 140

Young Anchoragites take part in an outhouse race during the Fur Rendezvous.

The Eskimo blanket toss is a favorite event of young people.

events remind Anchoragites of how the city's early settlers had to deal with harsh winter weather. Auctioneers sell fox, beaver, bear, and other furs that were once used to make warm winter clothing. The World Championship Sled Dog Race begins on a snow-covered downtown avenue. Other events are more modern—hot-air balloons lift off from Delaney Park, and Grand Prix racers roar through the streets.

Anchoragites enjoy themselves during the ten wintry days of Fur Rondy. They take part in nonsense events such as playing softball on snowshoes and running races with outhouses. Children especially like the Eskimo blanket toss, because they can be tossed from a blanket high

A brightly colored hot-air balloon rises over Anchorage during Fur Rondy.

nue downtown to watch mushers and their teams of twelve or more dogs start the 1,049-mile (1,689-kilometer) trek north to Nome. This trail was chosen in memory of the heroic mushers who in 1925 raced through extreme cold and snow to bring life-saving medicine to people suffering from a diphtheria epidemic in Nome.

The Iditarod is a cold and dangerous two-week journey through some of Alaska's most rugged mountains. In 1985, Libby Riddles became the first woman to win the race, and Susan Butcher won it in each of the next three years. The proud male mushers won back the title in 1989.

The city's many summer festivals allow residents to enjoy the beauty of Alaska's weather. On June 21, the Summer Solstice Festival celebrates the longest day of the year. This festival features a hot-air balloon race across the city, the Midnight Sun Balloon Classic, and an all-night softball tournament, where the lights are turned on for only two hours during the darkest part of the night. On the first Saturday following the solstice, runners from all over the world race in the annual Mayor's Midnight Sun Marathon.

Native Alaskans have celebrations of their own in Anchorage. During Quiana Alaska ("Thank you, Alaska") in mid-October, Eskimo and Indian peoples perform their traditional dances, wear native fur parkas, and tell stories from their past. Young people from throughout

These women help preserve the tradition of native Alaskan arts and crafts.

the state take part in the Alaska Native Youth Olympics in April. Special events in this competition include traditional native Alaskan contests such as the ear pull, the one-legged high kick, and the knuckle hop.

For the Anchoragite who likes indoor entertainment, the city provides a wide range of performing arts. Residents have been interested in the arts since the city began—Anchorage had an orchestra before it had paved streets. Today, the city has more than

75 arts organizations, including an award-winning repertory theater, a ballet company, and an opera. Special groups perform native Indian and Eskimo dances, and traditional Russian folk dances.

Anchorage has museums both big and small, which give residents and visitors the chance to learn more about the city's history, wildlife, and culture. The Anchorage Historical and Fine Arts Museum displays life-size exhibits of Indian houses, native clothing and arts and crafts, carved ivory sculptures, and an actual section of the Trans-Alaska Pipeline.

In the Alaska Wilderness Museum, visitors can come face to face with stuffed Alaskan wildlife. Grizzly bears, wolves, musk ox, dall sheep, and a beluga whale are all displayed as they would appear in their natural setting. In one exhibit, two black bears are shown ransacking a poor settler's cabin!

Anchoragites can see some of these same animals, and others as well, alive at the famous Alaska Zoo. Many are native to Alaska, such as bald eagles, snowy owls, arctic foxes, caribou, moose, and polar bears. Although these animals are at home in the wintry climate, the zoo's two elephants have had to learn to enjoy the snow. The privately owned Alaska Zoo was started when an Anchorage family won one of these elephants in a contest.

Two places downtown offer an unusual look at Alaska. In the Alaska

Experience Theatre, a wraparound movie screen surrounds viewers with the sights and sounds of the beautiful Alaskan countryside. The movie, which was filmed from an airplane, climbs mountainsides, dives through valleys, and chases caribou across an open plain. Viewers watching the film often feel as if they are in the airplane, too. Another exhibit recreates the earthquake that struck Anchorage in 1964, showing the damage on a screen while the floor rumbles and shakes beneath the seats.

The Imaginarium is a science discovery center that allows visitors to gain a hands-on understanding of science, nature, and technology. One exhibit takes people inside a bear's lair, where they can see how bears live and hibernate. In other exhibits, children can demonstrate scientific principles such as gravity or watch baby chickens hatch.

Although Alaska has no professional sports teams, Anchoragites enjoy plenty of sports action. Faithful fans go to games at the University of Alaska, Anchorage, to cheer for its basketball and hockey teams. In December, the UAA hockey team hosts the nation's toughest teams at an annual holiday hockey tournament. Every November, men's college basketball teams come from all over the United States to compete in the Great Alaska Shootout, held in the city's Sullivan Arena. In February, women's college basketball teams play in the Northern Lights Invitational.

Baseball fans can also enjoy this favorite American sport in Anchorage. The Anchorage Glacier Pilots compete in the Alaska Baseball League, a group of six state teams that ranks as one of the top amateur baseball leagues in the nation. The Anchorage team has won three national championships in the past twenty years, even though their season is only two months long.

Anchorage is known as a city for people who like to play sports as much as they like to watch them. More than 100 miles (161 kilometers) of biking and jogging trails run throughout the municipality. In the winter, cross-country skiers can be seen gliding along paths that run past Earthquake Park or along Turnagain Arm. Downhill skiing is popular in the nearby mountains—the municipality features three different ski areas, including Alyeska Resort and Ski Area with its beautiful view of Cook Inlet. In 1989, Alyeska's challenging runs were the site of the World Junior Alpine Championships.

During the summer, many visitors fly to the city to take fishing trips or helicopter sightseeing adventures in the state's vast wilderness areas. Other visitors board a train in Anchorage for the seven-hour trip to Denali National Park, where Mount McKinley is located.

Yet, there are many places within the municipality to view wilderness and wildlife. Potter Point State Game Refuge, on the southern edge of the

city, is home to more than 130 species of birds. People walk along its wooden boardwalks, and some try to photograph the birds that swim in the marsh below. Other nature watchers visit Ship Creek, north of downtown, to watch the salmon swimming upstream.

Adventuresome Anchoragites sometimes hike through the Chugach National Forest or go rock climbing in the mountains. Others like to pan for gold at historic Crow Creek Mine along Turnagain Arm. A half-hour drive farther south, people can view the sky-blue ice of Portage Glacier. Huge chunks of ice break off this 1,000-year-old glacier as it slowly melts and moves back into the mountains. Sometimes smaller pieces drift so close to shore that people can touch them.

A spirit of adventure is all it takes to enjoy Anchorage. This frontier spirit brings Anchoragites together in hard times and to celebrate the good ones. Their magnificent young city offers its people a lifetime of beauty and discovery.

Many visitors make the short trip from Anchorage to see majestic Portage Glacier.

Places to Visit in Anchorage

Downtown

Alaska Center for the Performing Arts
425 G Street
(907) 277-1988

Alaska Experience Theatre and Alaska Earthquake Exhibit
705 W. 6th Avenue
(907) 272-9076

Alaska Wilderness Museum
844 W. 5th Avenue
(907) 274-1600

Anchorage Museum of History and Art
121 W. 7th Avenue
(907) 343-4326

Imaginarium
725 W. 5th Avenue
(907) 276-3179

Oscar Anderson House
420 M Street
(907) 274-2335

Captain Cook Monument
Resolution Park
L Street between 3rd and 4th avenues

Delaney Park
Between 9th and 10th avenues, from A to P streets

Anchorage Bowl Area

Alaska Heritage Library-Museum
C Street and Northern Lights Boulevard
(907) 265-2834
Rare books, maps, paintings, photographs, native baskets, and artifacts

Alaska Zoo
4731 O'Malley Road
(907) 346-2133

Earthquake Park
Between Northern Lights Boulevard and Knik Arm

Ship Creek Salmon Overlook and Waterfowl Nesting Area
Whitney Road
During the summer, salmon can be seen swimming upstream here

Westchester Lagoon Waterfowl Nesting Area
Spenard Road, north of 36th Avenue

South Anchorage

Crow Creek Mine
Girdwood
Visitors can pan gold here

Potter Point State Game Refuge
Seward Highway
A wetland where more than 130 species of birds can be observed

North Anchorage

Eagle River Visitors Center, Chugach State Park
Mile 12 Eagle River Road
(907) 694-2108

Saint Nicholas Russian Orthodox Church and native spirit houses
Eklutna

Near Anchorage

Alyeska Resort and Ski Area
Seward Highway, 37 miles south of downtown
(907) 783-2222

Portage Glacier
Begich, Boggs Visitors Center
Seward Highway, 55 miles southeast of downtown
(907) 783-2326

Additional information can be obtained from these agencies:

Anchorage Convention and Visitors Bureau
201 East Third Avenue
Anchorage, AK 99501
(907) 276-4118

State of Alaska
Department of Commerce and Economic Development
Division of Tourism
P.O. Box E
Juneau, AK 99811
(907) 465-2010

Anchorage: A Historical Time Line

1778 — Captain James Cook is the first European to explore the Cook Inlet, near where Anchorage is today

1867 — The United States buys Alaska from Russia

1914 — The U.S. government decides to build a railroad in Alaska; the site where Anchorage is today is chosen as a construction headquarters; many job seekers travel to the tent city

1915 — The U.S. government sells homesites in the new town; the first frame houses are built

1920 — Anchorage incorporates as a city

1923 — The Alaska Railroad is completed

1940-41 — Fort Richardson and Elmendorf Air Force Base are built on the outskirts of Anchorage; the population triples in the next ten years

1951 — Anchorage International Airport opens

1957 — Oil is discovered in Cook Inlet

1958 — Alaska becomes the 49th U.S. state

1964 — The strongest earthquake in the history of the United States strikes Anchorage

1968 — Oil is discovered in Prudhoe Bay

1973 — The first Iditarod dogsled race is run

1975 — Anchorage joins with nearby smaller communities to form the Municipality of Anchorage

1981 — Pope John Paul II visits the city

1986 — Mount St. Augustine erupts in Cook Inlet, spilling ash over Anchorage

1987 — Unemployment reaches 11 percent after the price of oil falls

1989 — The *Exxon Valdez* runs aground in Prince William Sound

Index